# What to do when your mom or dad says... "YOU WANT A PET?"

By
JOY BERRY

GROLIER ENTERPRISES CORP.

Grolier Enterprises Inc. offers a varied selection of both
adult and children's book racks. For details on ordering,
please write: Grolier Enterprises Inc., Sherman Turnpike,
Danbury, CT 06816 Attn: Premium Department

## CREDITS

*Producer*
  Ron Berry

*Editor*
  Orly Kelly

BDOOTY9SU2

Have you ever asked your parents if you could have a pet only to have them say

There are many reasons why your parents might be cautious about you owning a pet. Some of them are that

- it costs money to buy the things a pet needs;
- it takes a lot of time and effort to take care of a pet;
- taking care of a pet is a big responsibility that lasts for the entire life of the pet.

Often children get tired of being responsible for their pets and stop taking care of them. When this happens, parents usually have to take care of the pets so they will not be neglected. Parents have many responsibilities. Most parents do not want the added responsibility of taking care of their children's pets.

If your parents are like most parents, they will *not* allow you to have a pet unless you make two promises.

**1. You must promise to be responsible for your pet for its entire life.** Being responsible for a pet means you will

- give your pet proper food and fresh water;
- give your pet an adequate, safe space in which to live;
- keep your pet's space clean;
- do whatever is necessary to keep your pet healthy and safe;
- do whatever is necessary to help your pet if it is sick or injured; and
- work with your parents to make sure that your pet's ability to have babies is controlled.

**2. You must promise that you will not expect other people to take care of your pet for you too much of the time.** Of course, you must be sure that another person is willing and able to care for it if you are not available. However, you, not other people, should provide most of your pet's care.

It will be easier for you to keep the promises you make to your parents if you choose the right pet for yourself. To choose the right pet, you should follow four steps.

## Step One: Consider your choices.

There are two kinds of pets from which to choose. The first kind is called a **short-term** pet. This is an animal captured in its natural environment. It is kept for a while and then returned to nature. Short-term pets include reptiles, amphibians, insects, and sea animals.

The second kind of pet is called a **long-term** pet. This is a domesticated animal, bred to be dependent on humans. If it is left on its own, it is unable to survive. Therefore, it is kept by its owner until it dies or is given to a new owner. Long-term pets include dogs and cats.

Here is a list of short-term pets:

Ants
Beetles
Caterpillars
Crabs
Crayfish
Crickets
Earthworms
Frogs
Iguanas
Lizards
Salamanders
Sea Animals

Skunks
   *(not legal to own
   in some states)*
Slugs
Snails
Snakes
Tadpoles
Tarantulas
Toads
Tortoises
Turtles

Here is a list of long-term pets:

Birds
Canaries
Cats
Chickens
Cows
Dogs
Ducks
Ferrets
   *(not legal to own
   in some states)*
Geese
Gerbils
   *(not legal to own
   in some states)*
Goats

Goldfish
Guinea Pigs
Guppies
Hamsters
Horses
Mice
Mynah Birds
Parakeets
Parrots
Pigeons
Rabbits
Rats
Tropical Fish

Some animals captured in the wild have diseases that can be given to the humans and animals they touch. Most animals captured in the wild can be extremely difficult to tame. For these reasons it is best not to capture and tame any wild animal without the assistance of a trained adult.

Once you have considered your choices, you are ready for the next step.

## Step Two: Learn about the pets you would like to own.

To learn about pets

- read books that you buy from bookstores or borrow from the library, and
- talk to pet owners, people who work in pet stores, and veterinarians.

Here is a questionnaire that will help you get all the information you need.

All about _____
(*Type of animal*)

### Life Span:
What is the normal life span of this animal?_____

### Living Conditions:
Should this animal be kept indoors or outdoors? _____
Should this animal be kept where it is warm or cold? _____
What kind of house or shelter, if any, does this animal need (cage, vivarium, aquarium, serpentarium, hutch, shed, coop, pen, fenced-in yard, etc.)? _____

### Diet:
What does this animal eat? _____
_____

### Care:
How often should this animal be fed? _____
How often does this animal need water? _____
How often should this animal's home be cleaned? _____
_____

12

What cleaning and grooming does this animal need? _____

_____

Should this animal be trained? _____

Should this animal be exercised? _____
    If so, how often? _____

Does this animal need immunizations (shots)? _____
    If so, what are they? _____

List other special requirements this animal may have. _____

_____

## Habits:
Does this animal respond positively to humans? _____
When and for how long does this animal sleep? _____

_____

At what time of the year is this animal most active? _____

## Illness:
What are common illnesses for this pet? _____

_____

How can these illnesses be avoided? _____
What will help cure these illnesses? _____

## Cost:
How much will it cost to buy this animal? _____

How much will the home and equipment for this animal cost?

_____

How much will it cost to feed and take care of this animal? __

_____

## Special Problems:
What special problems would owning this animal cause? ____

_____

Once you have learned about the pets you would like to own, you are ready for the next step.

## Step Three: Choose the right pet for yourself.

It is extremely important that you involve your parents in this step.

Share your research with them. Allow your parents to help you choose a pet that is right for you.

You and your parents might want to use this questionnaire to help you make your decision. If you can say that all of these statements are true, you have most likely chosen a pet that will be good for you.

Type of Animal _____

1. No one in my family is allergic to or terrified by this animal.
2. No one in my family will be bothered by the habits of this animal.
3. My family and I are aware of the special problems this animal might cause.
4. I can provide adequate living conditions for this animal.
5. I can provide an adequate diet for this animal.
6. I am willing and able to provide adequate care for this animal.
7. I am willing to do everything I can to help this animal if it is injured or sick.
8. My family or I can afford to buy this animal anything it needs to live a normal, healthy life.

Discuss with your parents any statement that is not true. There may be a way to compromise. If not, accept the fact that you should not have this particular animal.

Once you have chosen a pet, you are ready for the last step.

## Step Four: Obtain the pet.

Good places to get pets are

- certified breeders,
- reputable pet stores,
- animal shelters, and
- friends and neighbors.

Here are some other ways to find a pet:

- answer ads in the newspaper,
- respond to announcements on bulletin boards in local stores and public places, or
- talk to a veterinarian.

Soon after you get your new pet, you should take it to a veterinarian for an examination. Your pet will be checked for parasites like fleas, ticks, mites, and worms. It will also be checked for defects, infections, and illnesses. Your pet might be given necessary immunizations at this time.

The veterinarian will tell you all about your pet, including how to take care of it.

You should take your pet back to the veterinarian if it is ever sick or hurt. Your pet cannot tell you when something is wrong, so you must be aware of signs of illness or injury. Sick or injured pets act and look different from healthy ones. Watch for any of the following signs:

- bleeding anywhere on your pet's body,
- blood in your pet's bedding or in its bowel movements,
- runny nose or runny eyes,
- diarrhea or vomiting,
- limping or difficulty in moving around,
- lack of energy, listlessness,
- hiding,
- refusal to eat or drink,
- dull eyes,
- dull coat,
- ruffled feathers on your bird,
- warm, dry nose on your dog, or
- any unusual behavior.

Now that you know some general pet care, here are some specific instructions for taking care of five of the most common household pets:

## DOGS

**Before** you bring your dog home, you will need

- food (special puppy food if you are getting a puppy),
- a food dish,
- a water bowl,
- a bed or sleeping area,
- a collar,
- a leash,
- a brush,
- a comb, and
- toys for chewing.

**After** you bring your dog home, you will need

- an identification tag,
- the necessary shots, and
- a license.

## Diet for Dogs and Puppies

Every dog and puppy needs plenty of fresh water every day. In addition to water,

- puppies eight to twelve weeks old need four meals a day,
- puppies three to six months old need three meals a day,
- puppies six months to one year old need two meals a day, and
- dogs one year and older need one to two meals a day.

*Note:* The amount of food will vary according to the size and breed of each dog.

Dry or canned foods or a mixture of both with water or broth provide a well-balanced diet. Other foods may include

- cottage cheese,
- cooked egg,
- cooked vegetables, and
- animal vitamins.

Table scraps and real bones are not good for your dog or puppy.

## Housing for Dogs and Puppies

Puppies need an enclosed space for sleeping. A dog bed, dog house, or cardboard box can be lined with newspaper, an old blanket, or towel.

If your dog must sleep outside, be sure to provide a shelter that is large enough and gives adequate protection from the weather.

# General Daily Care for Your Dog

- Feed your dog and give it fresh water every day.
- Wash your dog's dishes every day.
- Keep your dog's bedding clean and dry.
- Keep outdoor areas used by your dog clean.
- Clean up after your dog in public places or on the property of others.
- Groom your dog by frequent brushing and bathing according to your veterinarian's instructions.
- Use flea products according to your veterinarian's recommendation.

## Special Needs of Dogs

• Purchase a dog license, and attach it to your dog's collar with an identification tag. The ID tag should include your dog's name, your name, your address, and your phone number.

• Train your dog when it's old enough to learn to obey. You can borrow a book on dog training from your local library or enroll your dog in an obedience class.

• Be sure your dog gets enough exercise for its size and breed. Large sporting dogs like retrievers need more exercise than small breeds like toy poodles. But all dogs need some exercise to stay healthy.

• Give your dog plenty of attention. Dogs need people more than people need dogs. Don't neglect your dog's need for human attention and contact.

Ask your parents to help you

- get your dog checked by a veterinarian at least once a year to maintain its health and update its shots;
- get veterinary treatment for your sick or injured dog;
- get your dog spayed or neutered when it is between six months and one year old.

# CATS

**Before** you bring your cat home, you will need

- food,
- a food dish,
- a water bowl,
- a collar,
- cat toys,
- a brush,
- a comb,
- litter, and
- a litter box.

**After** you bring your cat home, you will need

- an identification tag,
- the necessary shots, and
- a license. (Some states require this. Some states do not.)

Every cat needs plenty of fresh water every day. In addition to water,

- kittens six weeks to six months old need three meals a day;
- kittens six months to one year old need two meals a day; and
- cats one year old and older need one meal a day.

Ask your veterinarian to tell you the exact amount of food to give your cat or kitten. Dry or canned food made especially for cats will provide a well-balanced diet for your cat. Other foods may include

- dairy products such as milk and cottage cheese,
- boned fish, and
- animal vitamin tablets.

## Housing for Cats

Cats need a warm, dry place of their own, preferably indoors. Cats kept indoors are safer than cats allowed to roam outdoors.

## General Care for Your Cat

- Feed your cat and give it fresh water every day. Throw away any leftover wet cat food.
- Wash your cat's dishes every day.
- Keep your cat's bedding clean and dry.
- Clean your cat's litter box, and refill the box with fresh litter frequently.
- Keep the cat box in the same place, out of your family's way.
- Groom your cat regularly by brushing and combing it and checking its ears for mites.
- Regularly apply a flea product as recommended by your veterinarian.

## Special Needs of Cats

- Identify your cat with an ID tag attached to a safety collar. (A safety collar is a collar your cat can get free of if the collar gets stuck on something.) Your cat's ID tag should include your cat's name, your name, your address, and your phone number.

- Provide a scratching post for your cat to sharpen its claws.

Ask your parents to help you

- get your cat checked by a veterinarian at least once a year to maintain its health and update its shots;
- get veterinary care for your sick or injured cat;
- get your cat spayed or neutered when it is between six months and one year old.

# BIRDS

Each type of caged bird requires its own special care.
Check with your local pet store, veterinarian, or Society for
the Prevention of Cruelty to Animals (SPCA) for the special
needs of your bird. Parakeets make good pet birds and
require care that is similar to that of many caged birds.

*Before* you bring your parakeet home, you will need

- a cage,
- food dishes,
- water dishes,
- parakeet seed,
- a cuttlebone,
- grit or bird gravel, and
- toys.

# Diet for Parakeets

Your parakeet should be given fresh, clean water every day. In addition to water, your parakeet needs

- parakeet seed,
- grit or bird gravel,
- a cuttlebone for minerals and for beak care,
- bits of fresh, washed, green vegetables and fruits (occasionally),
- treat seed (occasionally), and
- vitamins (optional).

## Housing for Parakeets

Since your bird will spend all of its life in a cage, the cage should be large enough for it to live in. Wire cages that are about two feet by two feet by one-and-a-half feet are big enough for one or two parakeets. The cage should have

- perches,
- food and water dishes,
- a swing, and
- toys (such as a bell or mirror).

You may want to purchase a second, small cage to keep your bird safe when traveling with it, visiting the veterinarian, or while you are cleaning the larger cage.

## General Care for Your Parakeet

- Check your bird's food and water dishes every day. Make sure the seeds in the food dish are not empty hulls. Give your bird fresh water every day.
- Every two or three days,
  clean the food and water dishes,
  scrub the dirty perches and toys, and
  change the paper on the bottom of the cage.

Keep anything sharp or small enough to swallow out of your bird's cage. Place the bird cage

- out of the reach of small children, cats, and dogs; and
- away from air conditioners, heaters, drafts, and open windows.

## Special Needs of Parakeets

Parakeets like to have attention. They also like to "talk" and be talked to. You can train your parakeet to

- sit on your finger,
- spend time outside of its cage,
- sit on your shoulder, and
- repeat words and phrases.

You will need to work with your bird every day to teach it tricks. Be patient. Start teaching your parakeet to sit on your finger when you gently put your hand into its cage.

Repeat one or two easy words every day if you want your bird to learn to "talk."

## RODENTS

Guinea pigs, hamsters, mice, rats, and gerbils belong to a group of animals called rodents. These domesticated rodents are commonly kept as pets. Although each of these rodents is different from the others, they all have similar habits and need similar care. The guinea pig (also called a cavie) is typical of this kind of pet. Check with your local pet store, veterinarian, or SPCA for information on how to care for these animals.

**Before** you bring your guinea pig home you will need

- a cage,
- a water bottle,
- a food dish,
- food, and
- a box for sleeping.

## Diet for Guinea Pigs

Your guinea pig should have access to fresh, clean water every day. (A special water bottle attached to the side of a cage works best for guinea pigs.) In addition to water, your guinea pig needs

- specially prepared food pellets,
- citrus fruits (occasionally),
- leafy vegetables (occasionally),
- a salt lick,
- a block of wood (for chewing with its front teeth), and
- vitamins (optional).

# Housing for Guinea Pigs

Since your guinea pig will spend most of its time in a cage, the cage should be large enough for the guinea pig to be comfortable. Wire cages about two feet by two feet by two feet are big enough. The cage should have

- a board or shelf (to provide some relief from walking on the wire floor), and

- a covered sleeping box lined with shredded paper or cedar shavings (to satisfy your pet's nesting instinct).

A removable tray with cat litter that can slide under the wire floor makes cleaning the cage easier.

## General Care for Your Guinea Pig

- Be sure your guinea pig has food and fresh water every day.
- Remove any fresh food remains, like leafy vegetables, from your pet's cage every day. (Food pellets can be replenished as needed since they do not spoil.)
- Change the bedding in your guinea pig's sleeping box every day.
- Change the litter tray every other day.
- Groom a long-haired guinea pig by occasionally brushing its hair with a soft pet brush.
- Allow your guinea pig to move about outside its cage for exercise. Make sure you keep a careful eye on it while it is outside its cage.

## Special Needs of Guinea Pigs

- Make sure the diet you feed your guinea pig meets its special need for vitamin C.
- Handle your guinea pig often to keep it tame.

- Keep two guinea pigs or give your only guinea pig plenty of attention because they like companionship.
- If you have two guinea pigs, control their reproduction by making sure they are the same sex.

# FISH

Many kinds of fish can be kept as pets in home aquariums. Ask your local pet store or a tropical fish breeder about the needs of different kind of aquarium fish. Goldfish are a typical kind of fish kept in home aquariums.

**Before** you bring your goldfish home you will need

- a proper aquarium,
- fish food,
- water in the aquarium (which has been allowed to settle for at least two days),
- water plants or an air filter, and
- a small mesh fish net.

## Diet for Goldfish

Goldfish need a specially prepared dry goldfish mix. Here are a few tips for feeding your goldfish.

- Feed your fish only once a day.
- Feed your fish only as much food as they can eat in five minutes. (Do not overfeed your fish.)
- Remove any extra food from the tank with a mesh net.

## Housing for Goldfish

Goldfish need a rectangular aquarium or a fish bowl with a wide opening. The water surface of their bowl or tank should be exposed to as much air as possible. You can also provide air for your fish tank or bowl by attaching an air filter. An air filter will help keep the aquarium clean.

An aquarium will support five goldfish for each gallon of water it holds.

## General Care for Goldfish

Goldfish need a clean aquarium or bowl and the proper amount of food to remain healthy. To maintain your goldfishs' aquarium:

- Clean your fish bowl thoroughly at least once a week.
- Prepare a substitute fish bowl for your fish while theirs is being cleaned.
- Let the fresh water stand for at least two days in each of the bowls or aquariums before adding your fish.

## Special Needs of Goldfish

Goldfish are very sensitive. They can feel vibrations and smell and taste any changes in their water.

Whatever pet you choose, it is important to give it good care. If you do this, you'll have a good friend.